Beautiful, Wonderful You

A 30-Day Devotional to

Discovering Your Divine Design

By Jane Landers

ACKNOWLEDGEMENTS

I would like to thank my glorious King Jesus for His amazing love, forgiveness and for continuing to teach me who I am in Him. Without Him none of this would be possible.

I would like to thank my husband, Shane, for his patience, encouragement and support throughout this entire journey.

I would like to thank my dear friend, Emily Edwards, and her amazing friends, Heidi Tolliver, Gary Tolliver, and Fred and Valerie Paine for their hard work in making my book a reality.

I would like to thank my friend, Perla Perez Garner, for her continuous encouragement and support on writing this book.

CONTENTS

PROLOGUE

If I were to ask you today who you are, how would you answer? What character qualities describe you as a person and a woman? We each have deeply held beliefs regarding who we are. Some of them are true and accurate, and others not so much. The overwhelming majority of us prefer to see ourselves through rose-colored glasses. Often, this desire can be attributed to harsh life experiences or pain of one sort or another. When we have to admit imperfections, we struggle to come out of hiding—to deal with reality as it is.

Perhaps you've heard the phrase, "You must know who you are, but mostly you must know whose you are." The amazing truth is that while nothing is impossible for God, it's only when we come out of hiding and face the truth that he can do anything to change us. It's all about letting him shine a light into the dark cubbyholes of our lives and clean out the cobwebs that hinder the destiny he has for us.

During the next 30 days, you will be challenged to give God permission to search out the dark places inside you in order to change your perspective about who you are and how you fit into his marvelous plan. During this process, you—like a butterfly—will emerge with brand new insights into your identity in him. I pray that during our time together, you will discover the way he sees you and agree with him to become the beautiful creation you were meant to be.

> "'For I know the thoughts that I think toward you,' says the Lord, 'thoughts of peace and not of evil, to give you a future and a hope. Then you will call upon me and go and pray to me, and I will listen to you. And you will seek me and find me, when you search for me with all your heart. I will be found by you,' says the Lord, 'and I will bring you back from your captivity.'" (Jeremiah 29:11–14)

Before this journey begins, there are a few things I want to address. If you don't yet know Jesus Christ as your personal Savior and have never asked him to be a part of your life, I want to give you that opportunity today. All you have to do is to sincerely repeat the following prayer: "Lord, please come into my heart and take control. I receive you not only as my Savior, but also as my Lord. Forgive me for all the wrongs I've done and give me a heart to love and serve you in all I do and say. I ask this in Jesus' name, amen."

If you say this prayer, you can be certain that you will be saved. The Bible promises,

"If you confess with your mouth the Lord Jesus and believe
in your heart that God has raised him from the dead, you
will be saved." (Romans 10:9)

"For with the heart one believes unto righteousness, and with
the mouth confession is made unto salvation." (Romans
10:10)

If you've drifted away from the Lord and desire to get reconnected, please repeat this prayer: "Lord, I rededicate my life to you. Forgive me for growing cold and turning away from your love. Stir up the fire inside me so that I am once again passionate about you, yearning to be close the way I was when we first met. I ask this in Jesus' name, amen."

If you prayed this, then heaven is rejoicing, for Jesus said,

"What man of you, having a hundred sheep, if he loses one
of them, does not leave the ninety-nine in the wilderness,
and go after the one which is lost until he finds it? And when
he has found it, he lays it on his shoulders, rejoicing. And
when he comes home, he calls together his friends and
neighbors, saying to them, 'Rejoice with me, for I have found
my sheep which was lost!' I say to you that likewise there will
be more joy in heaven over one sinner who repents than over
ninety-nine just persons who need no repentance." (Luke
15:4–7)

If you have not received the Holy Spirit as your helper, you can do so now by simply saying: "Holy Spirit, I receive you into my life as my Helper and Comforter. I ask this in Jesus' name, amen."

> "But you shall receive power when the Holy Spirit has come
> upon you; and you shall be witnesses to me in Jerusalem, and
> in all Judea and Samaria, and to the end of the earth." (Acts
> 1:8)

If you prayed one of these prayers, why not write down today's date right now? This can be a great reminder of the day you received Christ or rededicated your life to him.

FOREWORD

You are about to embark upon the most rewarding journey of a lifetime – discovering how precious and valuable you are in the eyes of God. My prayer is that, as you apply these God-given principles, you will see the bigger picture of his great design for your life. Each day you will begin with a devotional reading followed by a Scripture, a challenge, a declaration, a prayer, and a time of meditation and journaling.

Daily Devotional Reading

Devotionals are written as an intimate "whisper" from God. As you sit in his presence and he speaks to your heart, you will respond with love and thanksgiving to the one who created and designed you as his masterpiece. Let him awaken you to your true identity in Jesus Christ.

> "He who dwells in the secret place of the Most High shall abide under the shadow of the Almighty. I will say of the Lord, 'He is my refuge and my fortress; my God, in him I will trust.'" (Psalm 91:1–2)

Daily Scripture

These Scriptures will help you apply God's Word to your life in a practical way. They are selected to give you God's perspective on each topic covered in this study.

> "This Book of the Law shall not depart from your mouth,
> but you shall meditate in it day and night, that you may
> observe to do according to all that is written in it. For then
> you will make your way prosperous, and then you will have
> good success." (Joshua 1:8)

Daily Challenge

Challenges reinforce what you have read and learned through the devotional and Scripture, giving you a creative means of applying truth to your life.

Daily Declaration

Declarations are to be spoken out loud for the purpose of coming into agreement with God's Word.

> "Death and life are in the power of the tongue, and those
> who love it will eat its fruit." (Proverbs 18:21)

Daily Prayer

Prayer is simply talking or communing with God. These prayers are designed to jump start and enhance your private time for expressing your thanks, confessing your weaknesses and sharing your requests with the Lord.

> "Be anxious for nothing, but in everything by prayer and
> supplication, with thanksgiving, let your requests be made
> known to God; and the peace of God, which surpasses all
> understanding, will guard your hearts and minds through
> Christ Jesus. "(Philippians 4:6)

Meditation and Journaling

While prayer is speaking to God, meditation is listening intently to hear his still, small voice and pondering his words. Consider reciting a verse of scripture as you color one of the designs. Journaling is for reflection, giving you an opportunity to record whatever insights you gained during the session.

> "I will meditate on your precepts, and contemplate your
> ways." (Psalm 119:1–2)

Famous Gems

During this journey, you will be introduced to the twelve gems on the breastplate worn by the high priests in Scripture. Just as birthstones vary in color and carry a specific meaning, you will learn the names, meanings, and godly principles behind each stone.

Understanding these gems is important because in 1 Peter 2 the writer identifies believers as a holy priesthood unto the Lord.

"But you are a chosen generation, a royal priesthood, a holy nation, his own special people, that you may proclaim the praises of him who called you out of darkness into his marvelous light; who once were not a people but are now the people of God, who had not obtained mercy but now have obtained mercy." (1 Peter 2:9–10)

As you discover the significance of each gem, may you be captivated by the Master Designer who created you as a colorful, intricate and beautiful design!

INTRODUCTION

Large tears rolled down Tia's five-year-old face as she ran out of the house. Although she couldn't quite make sense of it all, she had a relentless longing for her father's love and attention. Her father, a hard-working man who labored in the fields as a farmer and worked a second job as a lumberjack, lacked the ability to show love and affection to his children. Although he was a diligent man who made every effort to keep the family fed and clothed, he rarely spoke to his wife or children. The silence at times was painful, especially for young, sensitive Tia.

Tia quickly climbed up the apple tree in their front yard, where weeks earlier, she had arranged a few boards to sit on. It was the best a five-year-old could do to build a tree house of her own. It became her place of solace in a confusing world where she lacked her father's love and struggled to cope with a fearful, yet overbearing mother.

However, on this day something was about to change. It was as though the heavens had opened. She began to hear God whispering words of approval and love. Her Heavenly Father's kind and thoughtful words saturated her spirit and touched her longing heart. This encounter changed Tia. Now she knew that God was indeed her Heavenly Father.

Tears flowed, and her heart beat fiercely as the stunning revelation soothed her wounded heart. Although in the days and years to come, she would be tested regarding his unconditional love, that life-changing encounter made an impact she could not ignore. You see, God had a big plan for Tia's life, and nothing could stop his purposes and intentions. As the years passed, God strategically led Tia to others who would nurture her and remind her of God's plan for her life. Those precious people discipled Tia regarding her identity in Jesus Christ and reminded her that, above all, God loved her unconditionally.

Perhaps your life was vastly different than Tia's or maybe the wounds of the past have kept you from receiving God's love and embracing your true identity. I have good news for you today. No matter what your story, no matter where life circumstances have taken you, it is never too late to discover your identity as a child of God. My prayer is for you to open your heart and discover your true identity.

"The eyes of your heart may be enlightened in order that you know the hope to which he has called you, the riches of his glorious inheritance in the saints." (Ephesians 1:18 NIV)

Last of all, may your heart be healed and touched by the indescribable presence of God as you discover your identity as a daughter of the King, a divine design.

You Are About to

Discover

Your Divine Design

Day 1

A SPECTACULAR DESIGN

I was intentional when I created you. Please understand, my daughter, that your womanhood is not a biological accident. I desire for you to delight in the amazing wonder you are. You are strategically designed as a testimony to my character, reflecting the nature and reality of Christ. Therefore, I called you woman because you were taken out of man. You are made in my image, in my likeness, designed as a female to reveal the beauty and responsiveness to my voice as my redeemed bride, the church. As a bride, you fill a unique and special role as a loving support to your husband. I designed you to stand beside him to comfort, encourage and do him only good. You are perfectly fashioned and equipped for this good work as a gracious helper.

The husband's role is different than yours. My plan is for him to guide, protect, provide, and sacrifice for the family like my Son, Jesus.

As you discover and embrace the specific design I have laid out for you, your life will be one of greater joy and blessing. To truly understand your femininity, you must look to me to show you who you are. I've supplied you with beautiful examples in my Word to help you along the way to discovering your true self.

What a wonderful journey it will be as we walk hand in hand and I unveil the spectacular wonder of what it is to be truly feminine. I delight in your uniqueness, my daughter, so come and let's enjoy what I have created specifically for you.

Scripture:

"And the Lord God said, 'It is not good that man should be alone; I will make him a helper comparable to him.' Out of the ground the Lord God formed every beast of the field and every bird of the air, and brought them to Adam to see what he would call them. And whatever Adam called each living creature, that was its name. So Adam gave names to all cattle, to the birds of the air, and to every beast of the field. But for Adam there was not found a helper comparable to him and the Lord God caused a deep sleep to fall on Adam, and he slept; and he took one of his ribs, and closed up the flesh in its place. Then the rib which the Lord God had taken from man he made into a woman, and he brought her to the man." (Genesis 2:18-22)

Challenge: Re-read today's devotional message. On a Post-It note, write down two statements that stood out to you. Stick this note in a place where you can read it each day of your journey.

Declaration: "I am not a biological accident. I have a God-given role, and am created in my Father's image. I will delight in being a woman!"

Prayer: "Father, please help me grasp exactly what it means to be a woman created in your image. I want to embrace all that you have for me so I can see how unique and beautiful I am in your eyes. Strengthen me so that I can share with others what I've learned today. Thank you for designing me as a woman and allowing me to reflect your character wherever I go."

Meditation and journaling: Take the time to ponder this very important truth regarding your God-given role. Summarize your role according to the devotional and God's Word. Then write down one specific statement that stood out to you the most.

Notes

....

....

....

....

....

....

....

....

....

....

....

....

....

I HAVE A

God-Given Role

Day 2

COMPLETELY FORGIVEN

While I was on the cross, you were on my mind. I bore the punishment for all of the sins you would one day commit. You are forgiven because I chose to sacrifice my life for you. Accept the truth that when you ask me for forgiveness, I always forgive you and wipe away any memory of your sin. I see you as pure, radiant, and bathed in my righteousness alone. My child, I know your weaknesses, yet I gaze upon you with eyes of love.

Isn't this a freeing truth? Come to the one who knows you completely and loves you constantly. He desires to set you free from the heavy weight of guilt and shame. Is there a sin you need to confess and let go of today? Then, says the Lord,

"Come now, and let us reason together," Says the Lord, "Though your sins are like scarlet, They shall be as white as snow; Though they are red like crimson, They shall be as wool." (Isaiah 1:18)

Scripture:

"I, even I, am he who blots out your transgression for my own sake; and I will not remember your sins." (Isaiah 43:25)

Challenge: Imagine yourself on the hill of Golgotha with Jesus. Bring your sins, burdens and guilt and set them down at the foot of the cross. Look into the eyes of your savior and hear him say, "I forgive you." Now leave those weights there. Don't pick them up!

Declaration: "Because I have confessed my sins, I am forgiven! My Lord promises to wipe from his memory my sin and cleanse me from all unrighteousness. I am free—totally and completely free!"

Prayer: "Thank you for forgiving me and for washing me whiter than snow. Thank you for seeing me through eyes of love. Although this is difficult to comprehend, I choose to believe that I'm forgiven. When I sin, I will run to you to repent because your arms are always open to me. I love you, Lord. I am grateful for the way you love me! In Jesus' name I pray, amen."

Meditation and journaling: Take the time to meditate on the scene above. Write down your thoughts. Jot down the sins and burdens you laid at the foot of the cross.

Notes

UNDERSTANDING: SARDIUS

"And you shall put settings of stones in it, four rows of stones: The first row shall be a sardius, a topaz, and an emerald; this shall be the first row; the second row shall be a turquoise, a sapphire, and a diamond; the third row, a jacinth [ligure], an agate, and an amethyst; and the fourth row, a beryl, an onyx, and a jasper. They shall be set in gold settings." (Exodus 28:17–20)

In this day and age, the gem referred to in the Bible as sardius is called *sard*. This beautiful stone radiates an intense red with various shades of brown. Sardius was number one on the breastplate of the high priest, and it is one of the stones mentioned in the Book of Revelation as part of the foundation of the New Jerusalem. The name of this stone also means "to show blood." Since this stone is the color of blood, we can assume that it represents salvation by the blood of Jesus.

Sardius also represents the tribe of Judah, whose name means "I will praise." Once we receive salvation, we are thankful and desire to praise God for his amazing grace and mercy. Praise is our highest calling as children of God. Doesn't this make you want to shout and give him thanks?

"Praise the Lord! Praise God in his sanctuary; praise him in his mighty firmament! Praise him for his mighty acts; praise him according to his excellent greatness! Praise him with the sound of the trumpet." (Psalm 150)

Day 3

PASSIONATELY AND UNCONDITIONALLY LOVED

There is no love like my love. My love surpasses all understanding, especially in the fallen world in which you live. Although you may not have experienced unconditional love from your father, mother, or spouse, that doesn't change the fact that my love was there and is even now wooing you into my arms. Come to me and ask me to help you receive my unconditional love. You see, my child, I love you no matter what you've done or whether you feel it or not. My love is without conditions. Come to me and allow me to reveal my relentless love.

Scripture: "When I passed by you again and looked upon you, indeed your time was the time of love; so I spread my wing over you and covered your nakedness. Yes, I swore an oath to you and entered into a covenant with you, and you became mine,' says the Lord God" (Ezekiel 16:8).

Declaration: "My Father loves me! I am loved more than I can think or imagine. He looks beyond my faults and failures and loves what he sees. He genuinely loves me!"

Challenge: Share this profound truth with someone you know.

Prayer: "Lord, thank you, for loving me the way you do. Although I still struggle to believe you love me no matter how I perform on any given day, I'm beginning to see that your love is more than my mind can comprehend. Teach me how to receive your love so I can correctly love myself and others. I love you, Lord, for loving me. In Jesus' name I pray, amen."

Meditation and journaling: Write down what it was like living as a child growing up in your home. Did you believe you were loved and cared for? Whether your feelings are positive or negative, write them down. If there are any hurts, release them to the Lord by giving him the details and asking him to heal the wounded places in your heart. Color over all of the hurts with a red marker symbolizing they are covered by the blood of Jesus. Now ask him to fill those areas with his truth and give you the ability to receive his unconditional love.

Notes

Day 4

GRACE IS A GIFT

My child, please do not attempt to earn what is given to you freely as a gift. My grace is unmerited favor, available to you twenty-four hours a day. Stop struggling to do and say the "right" things. Take the "work" out of trying so hard to please me or others. Allow my grace to transform you from the inside out. Remember that where you are weak, I am strong. Receive all that I have for you by reaching out for my grace. Let it be moment by moment, if you must. Let go of unrealistic expectations of perfection. I am here with open arms to help you reach your potential in me. My grace is sufficient for you.

Scripture: "He said to me, 'my grace is sufficient for you, for my strength is made perfect in weakness.' Therefore, most gladly I will rather boast in my infirmities, that the power of Christ may rest upon me" (2 Corinthians 12:2).

Challenge: Ask yourself what makes you feel unworthy to receive God's grace. Be honest. Now, using a crayon, write your feelings on a mirror. Ask God to take away this sin and the feelings of unworthiness. Now wipe those words off the mirror.

Just like you physically wiped the words from the mirror, God has spiritually wiped away your sin and unworthiness. He erased them from his memory—wholly and completely—once you released them to him.

Declaration: "Grace is a gift! I will choose to receive his unmerited favor twenty-four hours a day!"

Prayer: "Heavenly Father, I know now that your grace can't be earned since it was freely given as a gift. Help me to receive it wholeheartedly so I can be free from performance and people-pleasing. Thank you for your mercy and your amazing grace. In Jesus' name I pray, amen."

Meditation and journaling: Take a moment to be still. Press in to hear God's voice. Ask him to show you how he sees you. What did he say to you? Journal his encouraging words.

Notes

....

....

....

....

....

....

....

....

....

....

....

....

....

....

....

Day 5

ADOPTED INTO GOD'S FAMILY

Dear daughter, the day you asked me into your heart, I sealed you with the Holy Spirit of adoption. This means that you belong to me, and nothing and no one can take you away from me. Your adoption also means you have an eternal home waiting specifically for you, filled with inexpressible joy. Never question whether you are mine. You are safe in my arms to be loved and cared for in ways you cannot even comprehend right now. Receive me as your Father, the one who loves you completely without restrictions. Call out to me, "Abba, Father," meaning you acknowledge me as your dear parent, both father and mother. Now, crawl up onto my lap. Allow me to speak words of love and comfort to your weary soul. You are always safe with me.

Scripture: "Having predestined us to adoption as sons [and daughters] by Jesus Christ to himself, according to the good pleasure of his will, to the praise and glory of his grace, by which he made us accepted in the beloved" (Ephesians 1:5-6).

Challenge: Close your eyes for a moment and picture yourself as a young child walking into God's presence. Allow the Lord to lift you onto his lap as a pure expression of his fatherly love for you. Listen to him say, "I choose you. You are my daughter. I will never leave you or forsake you, and no one can take you away from me."

Declaration: "The Lord says I am his daughter! I've been adopted into his family! He will never—no, not ever—leave me!"

Prayer: "Father, I come before you as your child, eager to receive and live according to the destiny you designed for me. I believe you are my Father. I am completely and totally yours. In Jesus' name I pray, amen."

Meditation and journaling: Re-read the challenge today. Write down the specific emotions you experienced. Be specific. Are you getting a clearer picture of the one you belong to?

Notes

Day 6

MORE THAN ENOUGH

Do you realize you are more than adequate? You might ask, "Why is that?" You see, my child, you were created in my image. You were formed in the very likeness of me. I created you with purpose and beauty and equipped you with everything you need to fulfill my purpose for you. However, you tend to compare yourself to others, and the devil uses this to speak evil, negative judgments about you that don't originate with me. Why do you want to compete with others who are also created in my image? When I look at you, I see an ocean of possibilities, a design intricately woven to portray loveliness and virtue, all unique to you. You are one of a kind. No one else has your fingerprints or talents or personality. You are perfect in my eyes. Now lift your head high and be thankful for who you are.

Scripture: "I will praise you, for I am fearfully and wonderfully made; marvelous are your works, and that my soul knows very well" (Psalm 139:14).

The word "fearfully" in this verse is actually translated from the Hebrew "to inspire awe". God didn't just make you – He made you wonderfully.

Challenge: Open your hands with palms up. Take a look at your fingerprints. Consider for a moment that there is absolutely no one else in the world with those same fingerprints. You are one of a kind!

Declaration: "I am more than adequate. My Father says I'm unique and one of a kind! I will praise him, for I am wonderfully made!"

Prayer: "I'm sorry, Lord, for all the times I had ugly thoughts about myself or felt jealous of other women. I give you my feelings of inadequacy and ask you to help me use the authority you've given me to say "no" to lies and negative emotions. Teach me to respect the truth that I'm created in your image. Thank you for showing me that I can be who you made me to be. In Jesus' name I pray, amen."

Meditation and journaling: Take a few moments to meditate on the truth that you're more than adequate according to Psalm 139:14. Is that hard for you to believe? Write down your thoughts. Now replace any negative thoughts with this truth: "I am an ocean of possibilities with an intricate design. I am lovely and valuable. I am unique."

Notes

Day 7

CHOSEN AND PREDESTINED

Long before I laid down earth's foundations, I had you on my mind. You were the focus of my love and affection. I wrapped you in my love through my Son, Jesus, so you would be holy and without guilt or shame. You are chosen, predestined, and adopted into my family for good works and for the pleasure of my will. Because of this, your future is brighter than any star in the universe. Allow your heart to soar above any feelings of loneliness or despair. You are mine—blessed, protected, and marked with a heavenly inheritance of spiritual blessings. Now come to me, and let us celebrate the truth that I've chosen you and adopted you into my family. My child, you are no longer alone.

Scripture: "For you are a holy people to the Lord your God, and the Lord has chosen you to be a people for himself, a special treasure above all the peoples who are on the face of the earth" (Deuteronomy 14:2).

Challenge: On a piece of paper, post this truth: "I am God's focus of love and affection. I've been adopted into his family, and I have a bright future." Hang it where you can see it to remind yourself of who you are in Christ Jesus.

Declaration: "I've been chosen, predestined, and adopted by God. I will not carry guilt or shame. I am a part of God's family, and my future is bright!"

Prayer: "Help me believe you have chosen me and set me apart for good works. Teach me the deeper meaning behind being adopted into your family. Help me remember that I'm never alone."

Meditation and journaling: Take time to meditate on the following statement: "Your future is brighter than any star in the universe." What words or pictures come to mind when you read that? Sketch or jot them down.

Notes

UNDERSTANDING: DIAMOND

"And you shall put settings of stones in it, four rows of stones: The first row shall be a sardius, a topaz, and an emerald; this shall be the first row; the second row shall be a turquoise, a sapphire, and a diamond; the third row, a jacinth [ligure], an agate, and an amethyst; and the fourth row, a beryl, an onyx, and a jasper. They shall be set in gold settings." (Exodus 28:17-20)

The diamond is one of the most sought-after gems today because of its rarity, beauty, and hardness. This beautiful gem glimmers, reflecting a rainbow of colors when held in the light. The Hebrew meaning of "diamond" is "a precious stone." The Lord refers to us in Scripture as "living stones" (1 Peter 2:5) being built up as a spiritual house and a royal priesthood for his glory.

The diamond was assigned to the tribe of Gad. Gad means a "troop cometh". The men of this tribe were known to be fierce, brave men of war who lead the children of Israel into the Promised Land. As children of God, we battle not against flesh and blood, but against spiritual hosts of wickedness. We are called to be fierce, brave warriors prepared to stand against the wiles of the devil armed with supernatural weaponry. "God's Word is an indispensable weapon. In the same way, prayer is essential in this ongoing warfare." As believers, we lead the way into the "Promised Land" by boldly sharing our testimony with others.

God's people are like diamonds with a clarity and strength that enables them to overcome whatever struggles come their way. That invincible, victorious spirit reflects God's anointing as a mighty troop coming forth.

Just like a flawless diamond, we glimmer, shine, and reflect his character. That's what I call priceless!

Day 8

A HEALED HEART

My daughter, who are you holding captive in your heart due to unforgiveness? It's time to release both yourself and the perpetrator by choosing to forgive. Remember, forgiveness is a choice. As you make the choice to forgive, I will give you the strength to overcome.

Everyone has pain, but it is what you do with the pain that matters. Whether you believe it or not, you alone are responsible for holding onto your pain, not the perpetrator. Unforgiveness will hinder you from becoming your true beautiful self. Once you choose to let go and release those things to me, I will work on your behalf. After all, I alone am the judge.

My thoughts are higher than your thoughts, and I know what is best. Search deep within to recall those who have offended you and caused you great pain. Ask the Holy Spirit to help you remember them one by one. When you fail to forgive them, your mind and emotions are tormented and held captive, but I have given you love, power, and a sound mind to free you.

The pain you hold so tightly is not yours to bear. I bore your griefs on the cross; therefore, they are no longer yours. The only person held captive with unforgiveness is you! Come, let us reason together; though your sins be as scarlet, allow me to wash them whiter than snow. I desire for you to be free and whole so that when you see your offenders, you are able to respond in love. This is a marvelous place to be and will keep you free from the sorrow of offense in the future.

Learn from me, for I am meek and gentle in heart. Here you will find rest for your weary soul. I love you, my child. We can do this together as you collaborate with me for your complete healing.

Scripture: "Whenever you stand praying, if you have anything against anyone, forgive him, that your Father in heaven may also forgive you your trespasses" (Mark 11:25).

Challenge: On a sheet of paper, write down the names of the people and the offenses that took place. Release them to the Lord by saying out loud, "I choose to forgive [use their name or names], so help me, Holy Spirit, to let them go." Now color over the offenses with your red marker symbolizing they have been covered by the blood of Jesus.

Declaration: "With the Lord's help, today I choose to forgive! I want to be set free and healed of every offense committed against me from this day forward. I let them go. I can do all things through Christ who gives me strength."

Prayer: "Lord, please forgive me for holding [name/names] captive and guilty in my heart. I want complete freedom from the offense [or offenses], so I'm asking for your help. Although I may not feel it, I'm now making the choice to let it go once and for all. Give me the courage to do what you are asking me to do without lingering resentment. Your spirit within me gives me the desire and power to forgive my offenders. You said to love our enemies and bless those who despitefully use us. Empower me to obey your decree. Thank you, Lord, for freedom and for loving me the way you do."

Meditation and journaling: Take time to think about the truth revealed to you today. Write down the way things appear from this perspective. Do you sense a change in yourself? If so, make a note. For instance, do you feel lighter and not so heavy? Now take the list you wrote in the Challenge and burn it as a prophetic act of faith, believing that it is no longer a part of you. Say out loud, "These offenses are gone, washed away by the blood of Jesus."

Notes

....

....

....

....

....

....

....

....

....

....

....

....

....

....

A note from the author: I want you to know one of God's greatest desires is for you to be healed emotionally. Healing is always available, twenty-four hours a day. Please don't allow Satan to tell you otherwise or allow him to steal the freedom you have gained. I would also like to encourage you to find someone with whom you feel safe, such as a pastor or counselor, who can remind you that you are free and keep you accountable to the truth. God's Word tells us there is strength in numbers: "Though one may be overpowered by another, two can withstand him. And a threefold cord is not quickly broken" (Ecclesiastes 4:12).

> "The unconfessed pain is a pain that never gets healed. We are as sick as the secrets we keep." — William Paul Young, author of The Shack

UNDERSTANDING: ONYX

"And you shall put settings of stones in it, four rows of
stones: The first row shall be a sardius, a topaz, and an
emerald; this shall be the first row; the second row shall be a
turquoise, a sapphire, and a diamond; the third row, a jacinth
[ligure], an agate, and an amethyst; and the fourth row, a
beryl, an onyx, and a jasper. They shall be set in gold
settings." (Exodus 28:17–20)

The word "onyx" means "to blanch." Blanching is a process whereby
food, either vegetable or fruit, is plunged into boiling water and
immediately transferred into cold or icy water. This process is used to
soften, cook, or remove a strong taste.

Often, we find ourselves in situations in which we are uncomfortable
or even unbearable. A common phrase we use is "I'm in hot water."
God uses difficult situations to conform us to his image. Tough times
can soften our hearts and make us open to God removing offensive
character traits. Only our loving God knows how much heat we can
bear and when to plunge us into a time of refreshing.

Onyx was given to the tribe of Asher. The meaning of Asher is
"happiness" or "to prosper, be blessed and to move forward." Isn't it
wonderful to know that, although we will go through seasons of
blanching, we can rejoice, knowing God is working things out for our
good?

Today I Choose To
Forgive
My Offenders

Day 9

A Position of Royalty

You, my daughter, are a part of a royal priesthood. You are royalty because you belong to me, the King of kings. I have chosen you to make a difference in this needy world. Allow the Holy Spirit to open your spiritual eyes so you can see how I've called you to be a part of something bigger than yourself. Know beyond a shadow of doubt that I've equipped you with everything you need to fulfill this role, including bringing others alongside to support you. As this revelation unfolds, your heart will be enlarged to include those I've placed in your life. Proclaim me to others and stand in the gap for those who are crushed and wounded. You represent me to a world in desperate need of love and acceptance. Take your position in the court of the King by believing me, using your faith and keeping a humble servant's heart. My eyes are on you at this moment, cheering you on as a part of a holy priesthood unto me.

Scripture: "Coming to him as to a living stone, rejected indeed by men, but chosen by God and precious, you also, as living stones, are being built up a spiritual house, a holy priesthood, to offer up spiritual sacrifices acceptable to God through Jesus Christ" (1 Peter 2:4–6).

Declaration: "I am royalty! I am part of a royal priesthood. God has called me to be part of something bigger than myself. Therefore, I choose to be his representative to a hurting world. I will put on royalty and wear it as a graceful crown and garment."

Challenge: Since the color purple represents royalty, why not purchase an item of this color as a reminder that you are part of a royal priesthood?

Prayer: "Father, thank you for showing me that I am royalty. Even though this is hard to believe, incorporate this truth into my thinking. I desire to represent you well to those who need to hear the gospel. Give me sensitivity for those around me who need your love and encouragement. In Jesus' name I pray, amen."

Meditation and journaling: Spend a few moments reading the devotional section again. Meditate on the truths you've discovered. Write down the ones that stood out to you and why.

Notes

Day 10
CHERISHED MORE THAN YOU CAN IMAGINE

My daughter, remember when you held your little one in your arms for the first time or shared treasured moments with a loved one? I cherish our moments together in the same way! I long to hear your voice and have your full attention. My eyes are constantly fixed on you. Even when you turn aside and focus on other things, I am still here. Come to me. I will show you how deep, how wide, how high and how long my love for you really is. My thoughts toward you are always good. I know the number of hairs on your head. I am aware of when you lie down at night and when you rise up in the morning. You are cherished. You are loved more than you can imagine.

Scripture: "For no one ever hated his own flesh, but nourishes and cherishes it, just as the Lord does the church" (Ephesians 5:29).

Challenge: Look up the definition of "cherish." Write it down on a Post-It note and place it where you can see it at all times.

Declaration: "I am cherished. I am deeply loved by my Lord! Each day I have a deeper revelation of what it means to be cherished by God."

Prayer: "Thank you, Lord, for cherishing me the way you do. I want to comprehend the width and length and depth and height of your love for me. Help me to prioritize spending quality time with you. I cherish the wonderful moments we spend together. In Jesus' name I pray, amen."

Meditation and journaling: Take time to meditate on the precious times you held your little one in your arms or the cherished moments you shared with a loved one. Journal what those experiences mean to you. Now invite the Lord to show you his thoughts about you and write them down. "For I know the thoughts that I think toward you, says the Lord, thoughts of peace and not of evil, to give you a future and a hope." (Jeremiah 29:11) Make a list of the reasons you cherish your times with him.

Notes

Day 11

POSSESSING A BEAUTIFUL MIND

Negative thoughts do not come from me. They come from negative experiences and past hurts or the evil one. If you live out your negative thoughts, they will eventually destroy the destiny I have for you. Take hold of your God-given authority and rebuke the enemy when he sets his sights on you to attack. Come, dear daughter, I desire to heal you. Allow me to transform your thoughts and sync them up with mine. Fix your thoughts on whatever is true, whatever is honorable and worthy of respect, whatever is right and confirmed by God's word, whatever is pure and wholesome, whatever is lovely and brings peace, whatever is admirable and of good repute; if there is any excellence, if there is anything worthy of praise, think continually on these things [center your mind on them, and implant them in your heart]. When your focus is on me, you will fulfill your destiny.

Scripture: For "who has known the mind of the Lord that he may instruct him? But we have the mind of Christ" (1 Corinthians 2:16).

Declaration: "I declare in Jesus' name: 'I have the mind of Christ. I think like him, and I talk like him, because he dwells inside me. My thoughts are his thoughts. I choose to release negative thoughts about myself and others to him. I choose to give him my past hurts and failures so I can be free in my mind, will, and emotions. I will keep my mind focused on whatever is true, pure, right, holy, and good.'"

Challenge: Be intentional about searching out any past hurts and negative thoughts you have about yourself and others. Make a detailed list of these things and release them to the Lord by confessing them. Take the list and burn it as a prophetic act of faith, agreeing with the Lord that they are no longer a part of who you are.

Prayer: "Heal me, God, from my wounds and insecurity. Free me from the fears that engulf my thoughts and try to control my life. I give you my negative thoughts and ask you to help me to keep my focus on you. I submit my mind wholly to you, in Jesus' name, amen."

Meditation and journaling: Write down what you experienced as you released those negative thoughts. What is the Holy Spirit telling you now?

Notes

Day 12

GOD'S MASTERPIECE

You are my masterpiece, beautifully and wonderfully made. When I created you, I carefully added each detail to support the specific role I designed for you. Do not belittle yourself by speaking ugly words about your appearance, abilities or personality. My heart breaks when you use such words against yourself. The enemy initiates, repeats and torments you with these accusations. Reject those word curses and do not utter them again.

My daughter, please do not to conform to this world by trying to change your physical appearance in order to feel loved and accepted by others. You are a masterpiece. You are beautiful. You aren't supposed to be like anyone else. You are thoroughly and completely accepted and loved by me, your Creator. Cling to these truths.

Outward beauty fades; a rose is proof of that. True beauty comes from within. As you yield your heart to me, I will weave in you a gentle, quiet spirit with the thread of love to touch people's hearts.

Scripture: "I will praise you, for I am fearfully and wonderfully made; marvelous are your works, and that my soul knows very well" (Psalm 139:14).

Challenge: Read Psalm 139:14–16. Write these verses down on a piece of paper. Carry them in your purse as a reminder that you are God's masterpiece. Share them with a person you care about who can't see her true beauty.

Declaration: "I'm beautiful. [Your name] is God's masterpiece! I'm not a scribble or a rough draft. I am a breathtaking, beautiful masterpiece designed by God himself."

Prayer: "Forgive me for the times I've spoken ugly words about myself. I didn't realize I was judging you. Give me a deeper revelation of my unique design and your incredible destiny for my life. Help me receive your love and acceptance instead of looking for it elsewhere. Thank you for loving me the way you do. In Jesus' name I pray, amen."

Meditation and journaling: Re-read Psalm 139:14–16. Try to visualize God creating and forming you in your mother's womb. Journal your thoughts about the God of the universe specifically designing you inside and out to his exact specifications.

Notes

UNDERSTANDING: SAPPHIRE

"And you shall put settings of stones in it, four rows of stones: The first row shall be a sardius, a topaz, and an emerald; this shall be the first row; the second row shall be a turquoise, a sapphire, and a diamond; the third row, a jacinth [ligure], an agate, and an amethyst; and the fourth row, a beryl, an onyx, and a jasper. They shall be set in gold settings." (Exodus 28:17–20)

In Hebrew, this beautiful stone is called saper, meaning "to polish, scratch, and divide." As one looks into the deeper meaning of this word, you discover that this gem can be used to scratch other substances to either mark, count, or to speak out. Some ancient writings even suggest that the Ten Commandments were etched on stones made of sapphire. Each time this gem is mentioned in the Bible, it is a picture of beauty and demands respect.

In the same way, the Word of God is written upon our hearts and it changes the way we live. When we allow God to mold and transform us, everyone around us is affected in a positive way. We have a guarantee in God's Word that we go from glory to glory. The most beautiful people are those whose beauty comes from within. God uses everything we go through to carve the likeness of Jesus in us until we love like Jesus, forgive like Jesus, and obey like Jesus. Now that's what we call true beauty!

Sapphire represents the tribe of Simeon, which means "God has heard" or "God hears." God does hear our prayers, and he is attentive to our voice. However we often do a lot of asking and talking but neglect listening—hearing God's voice. Is there anything more valuable to a child of God than hearing God's thoughts and desires? May we share our hearts with our Heavenly Father and develop listening ears to hear his heart. Now, that's what we call relationship!

Day 13

YOU ARE NOT ALONE

Do you realize that feelings of abandonment stem from the lies of the devil spoken into your heart? Satan was, and still is, a liar who plants seeds of confusion and turmoil. Never doubt that I am with you, dear child. I have promised, "I will never leave you or forsake you. Come to my throne of grace to receive mercy and help in time of need." I see your struggle and your attempts to fix yourself. I am the only one who can truly restore what the enemy has stolen. Although you may have been abandoned and neglected by others, I am here with open arms to receive you. Cling to me and let go of the yearning for someone other than me to fill that void. They cannot satisfy the way I can. Make the choice to shift your focus to me, and I will begin to reveal to you who I am in ways you never thought possible. I am your comforter, friend, helper, and the place of rest for your weary soul.

Scripture: "Let your conduct be without covetousness; be content with such things as you have. For he himself has said, 'I will never leave you nor forsake you'" (Hebrews 13:5).

Challenge: Take a moment right now and picture yourself sitting with Jesus. See with your spiritual eyes how attentive he is toward you. Allow this heavenly image to encourage your heart.

Prayer: "Father, help me discard feelings of abandonment and the orphan spirit. I realize that they are lies from the enemy. I choose to cling to you instead of clinging to others for acceptance. Thank you for caring for me the way you do and for your sweet, attentive voice. In Jesus' name I pray, amen."

Declaration: "I am not alone because the Lord is with me! He will never abandon me! Regardless of how I feel, he is with me. He is closer than the air I breathe, and I take great comfort in that knowledge."

Meditation and journaling: Meditate on the scene in the Challenge today. What else do you see or hear as you sit next to Jesus? What message of love and encouragement does Jesus give you? Write these things down in detail. Ask the Holy Spirit to lead and guide you.

Notes

Day 14

MORE THAN A CONQUEROR

Why are you fighting the enemy in your own strength? As your Savior and Deliverer, I have already won the battle. I have never asked you to strive or work at deliverance or breakthrough, but I do ask you to come alongside and agree with what I've already provided. Come to me and I will give you rest. Let me teach you, and you will find rest for your soul. I shed my blood and gave my life so you can live a life of victory. Stop struggling, and believe the enemy is already defeated. You are to fight by simply declaring and decreeing what I have already said. Pick up your crown and reign by speaking who you are in me. You are victorious! You are a conqueror! You can do all things because your strength is found in me!

Scripture: "Thus says the Lord to you: 'Do not be afraid nor dismayed because of this great multitude, for the battle is not yours, but God's'" (2 Chronicles 20:15).

Challenge: Write down Scriptures that describe your identity in Christ and hang them around your house to read on a regular basis. (These verses will get you started: John 15:15, Isaiah 49:16, Philippians 3:20, 2 Corinthians 5:17, Ephesians 1:3-8.)

Declaration: "I can have victory because Christ made a way for me through his work on the cross. I am not defeated, but an overcomer because I belong to the King of kings. He will fight for me!"

Prayer: "Father, forgive me for the times I've operated on my own to achieve a breakthrough. I realize the battle has been won, and the victory is mine because of your great work on the cross. Help me to walk out the rest of my days in agreement with your Word so I can live in victory. Thank you for your selfless sacrifice that made a way for me to be victorious. In Jesus' name I pray, amen."

Meditation and journaling: Think about the times you strived for a breakthrough in your life. What were the challenges you experienced and how did you handle them? Did you handle them well? Did you handle them poorly? What was the outcome? What would you do differently next time? Write down the main truths you discovered today. How will you react next time you need a breakthrough? Write that down as well.

Notes

UNDERSTANDING: LIGURE

"And you shall put settings of stones in it, four rows of
stones: The first row shall be a sardius, a topaz, and an
emerald; this shall be the first row; the second row shall be a
turquoise, a sapphire, and a diamond; the third row, a jacinth
[ligure], an agate, and an amethyst; and the fourth row, a
beryl, an onyx, and a jasper. They shall be set in gold
settings." (Exodus 28:17–20)

Ligure is mysterious to say the least. There is very little historical
evidence of this stone's existence. The term ligure is used twice in the
Bible, and both times in the context of the breastplate of the high
priest. There is a theory that ligure may be linked to a variety of
jacinth and zircon stones. These gems are either a fiery golden color
or blue, much like the burning sulfur described in Revelation 9:17.
When rubbed or heated, these stones take on an "electric" quality.

Ligure was the stone given to the tribe of Ephraim, which means
"double fruit." When we combine the meaning of the two, we get the
sense of attraction and double blessing. Jesus in us is the electrical
attraction that woos others, and ligure is a beautiful reminder of how
truly we are blessed.

I BELONG TO THE
King of Kings

Day 15

CONFIDENT AND COURAGEOUS

My child, I see fear preventing you from becoming the person I created you to be, preventing you from receiving my precious promises. I see the thoughts that rage in your mind. Thoughts that say, "If I do this, I'll look stupid." "What if I fail?" "Will people say, 'Who does she think she is?'" This battle goes on inside you day after day.

I see what's in your heart and your unfulfilled dreams. I know very well that in the deep recesses of your soul, you want to break free and find your niche, the destiny for which I made you. In order to find courage, you must first call out to me and let me show you a better way—my way. I am your confidence and the place where those dreams originated. How sad it would be to see you in heaven, knowing you never obtained the blessings you were entitled to on earth. Why not take one baby step toward becoming your true self? Reach out to me for the courage you need, then lean on me as you step out in faith and begin to accomplish what's in your heart.

Scripture: "I can do all things through Christ who strengthens me" (Philippians 4:13).

Challenge: First, write down your dreams. Ask the Lord to show you someone with whom you can share them (but make sure this individual is safe to confide in). Take the time to share your heart and ask that person to pray in agreement with you.

Declaration: "The Lord is my confidence! He is my strength and will deliver me from insecurity, helping me learn how to trust him! He will fight for me and give me the courage to step out in faith."

Prayer: "Lord, reveal to me my insecurities and the past failures that hinder me. With your help, I choose to let those things go. From this moment on, I choose to lean on you for the courage and strength I need to take steps of faith in the area you are putting on my heart. In Jesus' name I pray, amen."

Meditation and journaling: Read Philippians 4:13 out loud several times. Meditate on it. Write down what this Scripture means to you today. Replace the word "I" with your first name.

Notes

UNDERSTANDING: JASPER

"And you shall put settings of stones in it, four rows of stones: The first row shall be a sardius, a topaz, and an emerald; this shall be the first row; the second row shall be a turquoise, a sapphire, and a diamond; the third row, a jacinth [ligure], an agate, and an amethyst; and the fourth row, a beryl, an onyx, and a jasper. They shall be set in gold settings." (Exodus 28:17-20)

In Hebrew, "jasper" means "to polish." When this gem is polished, it reveals a beautiful inner quality. God knows we need polishing to reveal godly inner qualities, so he works with us gently over time to remove the sin and rough edges from our lives so we begin to shine with his glory.

Jasper was given to the Naphtali tribe. Naphtali means "my wrestlings." Our biggest battles are the wrestlings we undergo daily of choosing whether we will live for God or ourselves. Paul noted his great struggle in Romans 7:24-25, "Is there no one who can do anything for me? Isn't that the real question? The answer, thank God, is that Jesus Christ can and does. He acted to set things right in this life of contradictions where I want to serve God with all my heart and mind, but am pulled by the influence of sin to do something totally different." We all face these wrestlings, but praise the Lord "we can do all things through Christ who gives us strength", even overcome our flesh (Philippians 4:13)!

I Can Do All Things
Through Christ

Day 16

A RADIANT JEWEL

I see you as a precious jewel, my daughter. You are rare, beautiful, and radiant. I have adorned you with my love and grace. Some day when we see each other face to face, you will understand how valuable you are to me. Until then, allow me to reveal the glorious wonder of my light within you. Shine for me as you go about your daily tasks, displaying my love to all who meet you. You are fully equipped to give hope and encouragement to those around you. Etch these truths on your heart today and be seen as the exquisite jewel you truly are. You're beautiful—one of a kind! Shine, my daughter, shine!

Scripture: "They shall be mine," says the Lord of hosts, "On the day that I make them my jewels. And I will spare them as a man spares his own son who serves him" (Malachi 3:17).

Challenge: Consider a piece of jewelry or an item that reminds you of the jewel you are. Use this as a reminder that God sees you as beautiful and valuable.

Declaration: "The Lord calls me a precious jewel! I am his, and his light is within and upon me! By the power of the Holy Spirit I will shine for him!"

Prayer: "Lord, give me a clearer understanding of my value. I open my heart to receive your kind words. Shine like a jewel by loving others through me. I want to shine for you! In Jesus' name I pray, amen."

Meditation and journaling: Think for a moment of how the Lord sees you as rare, beautiful, radiant, and filled to overflowing with God's love and grace. What does that mean to you? Write down your thoughts.

Notes

UNDERSTANDING: EMERALD

"You shall put settings of stones in it, four rows of stones:
The first row shall be a sardius, a topaz, and an emerald; this
shall be the first row; the second row shall be a turquoise, a
sapphire, and a diamond; the third row, a jacinth [ligure], an
agate, and an amethyst; and the fourth row, a beryl, an onyx,
and a jasper. They shall be set in gold settings." (Exodus
28:17–20)

Emerald is well known specifically for its exquisite green color. It also
represents the season of spring and new birth. The Hebrew meaning
of "emerald" (nopek) means "to shine or glisten."

Although it appears to be a hard stone, the emerald is delicate in
nature and sensitive to detergents. One must be extremely careful not
to destroy the value of this precious gem by mistreating it. Our loving
Father treats us the same way. He knows our value and is careful to
protect us from harm. He lovingly cares for us, knowing how much
we can bear, and if we are tempted, he will always make a way of
escape. We can shine for him in spite of any challenge we may face.

Emerald was given to the tribe of Levi as a sign of their devotion and
God-given wisdom. Many sources say they were chosen by God to be
his priests because of their obedience to God after the fateful "golden
calf" episode at Mt. Sinai. There's no doubt that our devotion to God
will be tested. The question is, "Will we pass the test so that even in
the darkest of nights our light will shine for him?"

"No temptation has overtaken you except such as is common to man; but God is faithful, who will not allow you to be tempted beyond what you are able, but with the temptation will also make the way of escape, that you may be able to bear it." (1 Corinthians 10:13)

THE LORD CALLS ME
His Precious Jewel

Day 17

FILLED WITH GLORIOUS LIGHT

My dear daughter, you are light to a dark world. My light, the glory of my presence, is in and upon you. Once you accepted my gift of salvation, I came to live within you. Share my light with those who are in desperate need of hope and love. Do not hide this light within you. If you lack courage, seek me with all your heart. I promise to enable you to share the gospel in ways you never thought possible. If you are timid and hide your light, you are not being true to your real self or to me. I am the light of the world, and you are in me and I am in you; therefore, let your light shine for all to see. Come and let me show you how.

Scripture: "Let your light so shine before men, that they may see your good works and glorify your Father in heaven" (Matthew 5:16).

Challenge: Put a nightlight somewhere in the house to remind you that God has called you to be a light to a dark world.

Declaration: "I am a light. Christ shines through me! With the help of the Holy Spirit, I will let my light shine wherever I go and whatever I do."

Prayer: "Lord, give me a deeper revelation of what it truly means to have your light within me. Forgive me for the times I let fear stop me from sharing the gospel with others. Give me the courage to share the good news so I can be true to you and true to myself. In Jesus' name I pray, amen."

Meditation and journaling: Ponder the truth that you are to be a light to a dark world. Write down what that means to you or make a note to share your testimony (simply tell what God has done for you) with a friend.

Notes

UNDERSTANDING: CARBUNCLE

"And you shall put settings of stones in it, four rows of stones: The first row shall be a sardius, a topaz, and an emerald; this shall be the first row; the second row shall be a turquoise, a sapphire, and a diamond; the third row, a jacinth [ligure], an agate, and an amethyst; and the fourth row, a beryl, an onyx, and a jasper. They shall be set in gold settings." (Exodus 28:17–20)

Although no one really knows what the mysterious gem carbuncle is, many believe it is an emerald. Others think it is a red garnet. One thing we do know is that the Hebrew word root means "to glitter and flash." Sometimes it's hard for us to grasp the truth that we, as children of God, are like flashes of light to a dark world.

"…children of God without fault in the midst of a crooked and perverse generation, among whom you shine as lights in the world." (Philippians 2:15)

This stone was given to the tribe of Zebulun. The meaning of the name "Zebulun" is "to dwell." The second meaning is "exalted abode." What a glorious day it will be when the eastern sky will open and our Bridegroom calls us up to dwell with him forever!

"I will greatly rejoice in the Lord, My soul shall be joyful in my God; For He has clothed me with the garments of salvation, He has covered me with the robe of righteousness, As a bridegroom decks himself with ornaments, And as a bride adorns herself with her jewels." (Isaiah 61:10)

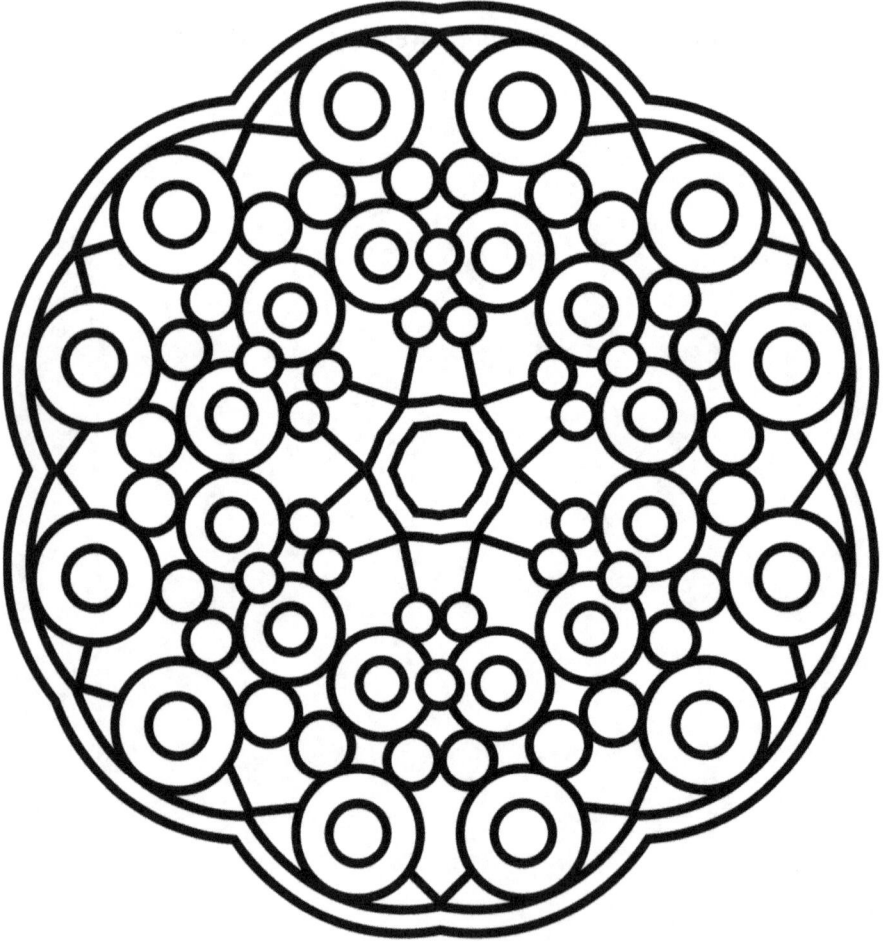

Day 18

DESIGNED TO BE DIFFERENT

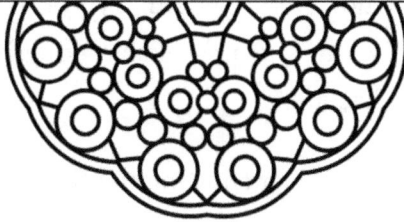

At times, I know you feel like a fish out of water. You sense deep down that you are different and don't always fit in with others. In one way, you're right. You're not of this world. In the depth of your very core, you're a spirit in a human body here on earth. You were created to be different, set apart for my purpose and glory. This means you must allow me to transform your mind as you read and think about the truth of my Word. It will grow like a seed inside you when you believe and apply it. When you nourish and treasure it, that seed will grow into a deeper understanding of my kingdom and your identity in it. You're right when you feel that you're not of this world, but that's only because you belong to an unshakable kingdom where you have everything you need pertaining to life and godliness.

Scripture: "Do not be conformed to this world, but be transformed by the renewing of your mind, that you may prove what is that good and acceptable and perfect will of God" (Romans 12:2).

Challenge: Look for and collect pictures of heaven on the internet. Although these are only man's idea of what heaven looks like, let them be a reminder that you are not of this world.

Declaration: "I am not of this world! I've been set apart for good works because I live in an unshakable kingdom where I have everything I need to live life."

Prayer: "Thank you, Lord, for showing me that I'm not of this world. I know that I was created for much more. Though I may struggle at times to believe this truth, I will apply your Word to my heart to transform my thinking so it lines up with who I really am. In Jesus' name I pray, amen."

Meditation and journaling: Read today's Scripture out loud several times. Write down the areas of your life where you have been conformed to the world and need to change. Journal what the scripture means to you and the steps you are willing to take in order to renew your mind.

Notes

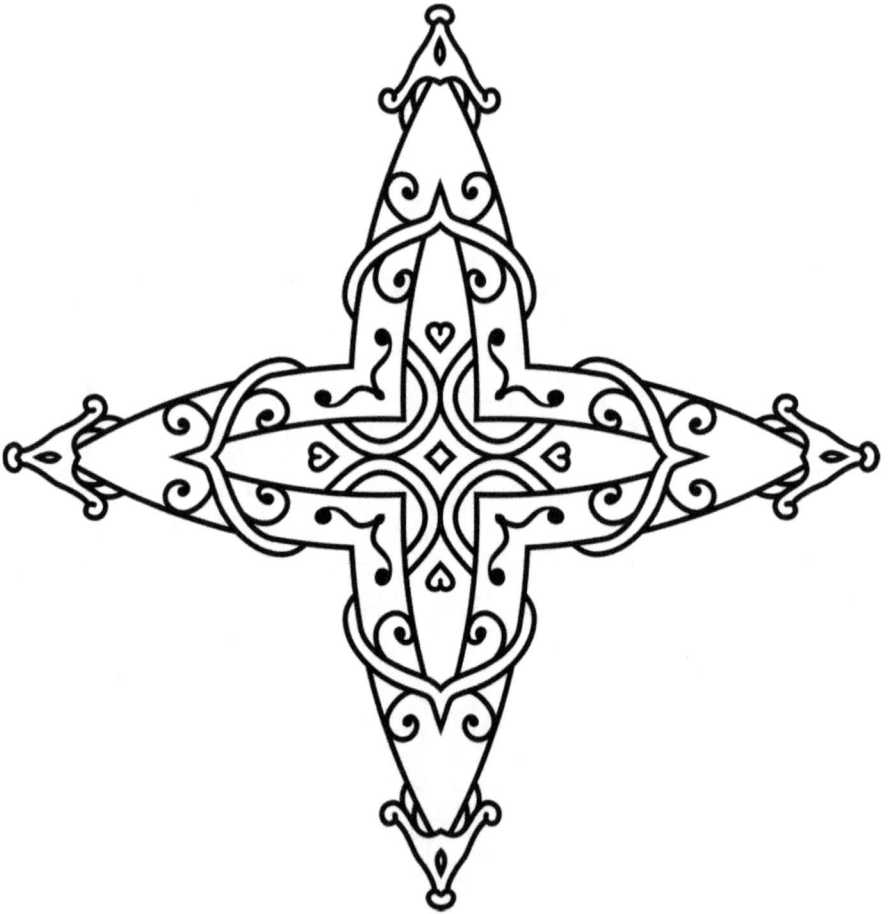

Day 19

GIFTED TO HELP OTHERS

Dear child, when I formed you in your mother's womb, I gave you a distinct personality and endowed you with many gifts, strengths, and talents according to my perfect will. Some of these gifts are from the Father. They empower and activate you in prophecy, ministry, teaching, exhortation, giving, leadership, and mercy. Some of these gifts are from the Holy Spirit. They empower and activate you in words of wisdom, words of knowledge, faith, gifts of healing, working of miracles, prophecy, manifestations of the Spirit of God, discerning of spirits, different kinds of tongues, and interpretation of tongues. Some of these gifts are from the Son. They are given to strengthen and equip the body of Christ. They include apostles, prophets, evangelists, pastors and teachers, and missionaries.

You are gifted and talented beyond anything you can comprehend. I will never take these precious gifts away from you. You, my daughter, have much to share. You are special, unique, and fearfully and wonderfully made, equipped for good works.

For more information and to discover your God-given gifts, you can go to www.giftstest.com

Scripture: "For the gifts and the calling of God are irrevocable" (Romans 11:29).

Challenge: Take a spiritual gifts test (such as those available on the Internet) to identify the gifts God has given you. If you have already done so, then consider whether you are using your God-given gifts. If not, review the meaning of your gifts and ask God to open the door for you to use them to bless others.

Declaration: "I am gifted beyond anything I can imagine because God has placed wonderful treasures inside me."

Prayer: "Thank you, Lord, for the gifts you've given me. Guide me as I learn to use them for your glory and not my own. In Jesus' name I pray, amen."

Meditation and journaling: Read again the different gifts God has given to his children. Which ones do you think belong to you? Write them down and journal your thoughts.

Notes

$\mathcal{D}$ay 20

COMPLETE ACCESS

Do you realize that you have complete access to the Father through me, your Savior, Jesus Christ? I paved the way for you to go before him in prayer by tearing down the wall of separation when I sacrificed my life on the cross. This does not come as a result of your self-righteousness, but comes through faith in me. You cannot earn or work for this holy privilege because you don't have the power to add anything to what I've already done. So now, my child, come boldly to the throne of grace where you can find mercy and help in time of need. Do not be anxious, but instead make your requests known to God in prayer, with a thankful and reverent heart.

Scripture: "For we do not have a High Priest who cannot sympathize with our weaknesses, but was in all points tempted as we are, yet without sin. Let us therefore come boldly to the throne of grace, that we may obtain mercy and find grace to help in time of need." (Hebrews 4:15-16).

Challenge: Is there a concern on your heart that you have been afraid to talk to God about or felt it was too insignificant to bring to God? Jesus sympathizes with your weakness, and he cares about everything that concerns you. Why not lift it up in prayer right now?

Declaration: "I have the awesome privilege of taking my requests before the Father because of Jesus. Nothing can keep me from coming to God's throne of grace!"

Prayer: "Thank you, Jesus, for tearing down the wall of separation between mankind and the Father. It is a holy privilege to come into God's presence. Let nothing hinder me from coming to the throne room. I have access to my Heavenly Father twenty-four hours a day."

Meditation and journaling: Take a few moments and think about today's devotion. Is it difficult for you to believe? Journal your thoughts and write a description of what it means to have personal access to the Father.

Notes

Day 21

DRESSED IN STRENGTH AND DIGNITY

I have placed on you a garment of strength. Although it is unseen in the physical realm, like the wind, it is there. My garment of strength gives you supernatural power to resist any temptation the enemy throws at you. Be wise and discern Satan's lies. You can do all things through me!

I've also clothed you with the glorious garment of dignity and self-respect. Wear this garment well and you will hold your head high without shame or guilt. When you come to me for forgiveness, I forgive you and remember your sins no more. Now take these truths and share them with others so they can hold their heads high and be the sons and daughters I've called them to be.

Scripture: "Strength and dignity are her clothing and her position is strong and secure; and she smiles at the future" [knowing that she and her family are prepared] (Proverbs 31:25 AMP).

Challenge: Find someone today with whom you can share these truths.

Declaration: "God has placed on me a garment of strength and dignity; therefore, I can resist whatever temptation comes my way! I am graced with nobility because I belong to the King of kings!"

Prayer: "Lord, with your help I can handle whatever comes my way. Show me how to build these truths in my heart so I can overcome any temptation. Give me keen discernment to know what I'm up against. Thank you for wrapping me in a garment of strength and dignity. With your help, I will hold my head high, knowing I belong to you. I no longer need to live in shame and guilt."

Meditation and journaling: What was the one thing that stood out the most to you in today's Challenge? Write down your thoughts and explain why.

Notes

UNDERSTANDING: AMETHYST

"And you shall put settings of stones in it, four rows of stones: The first row shall be a sardius, a topaz, and an emerald; this shall be the first row; the second row shall be a turquoise, a sapphire, and a diamond; the third row, a jacinth [ligure], an agate, and an amethyst; and the fourth row, a beryl, an onyx, and a jasper. They shall be set in gold settings." (Exodus 28:17–20)

The word "amethyst" means "to recover and to be healthy and strong." How beautiful it is to know that as we begin to understand God's love for us, we can literally improve our health – physically, emotionally, mentally and spiritually! His amazing love can recover every area of our lives.

This gem, amethyst, represents the tribe of Benjamin, which means, "Son of the right hand." Jesus, of course, is the "Son of the right hand" because he sits at the right hand of God.

Since he is God, he is also the one who makes all things right. Romans 8:28 says, he causes all things to work together for good.

How fitting for this stone to be purple in color! Purple is a sign of royalty. Jesus, the Royal One, clothed in purple, has clothed us in royal apparel and made us right with God.

I Am Clothed with
Dignity and Self-Respect

Day 22

GIVEN POWER, LOVE, AND A SOUND MIND

My child, fear does not own you. When you were born you had only healthy fears to keep you safe and secure. Tormenting, paralyzing fears are evil and reveal that your mind is focused on something other than me. Starting today, begin retraining your mind to focus on me and think my thoughts. There is no place for fear in my thoughts, for fear brings torment.

I've given you a spirit of power that will equip you to do what you cannot do by yourself. I've given you a spirit of love. Allow love to be your launching pad for everything you do, say and think. Love conquerors all. I've also given you a sound mind. A sound mind enables you to think clearly and rationally. My thoughts are filled with peace and stability. Come now, let me show you how to replace those fearful thoughts with my life-giving, peaceful thoughts.

Scripture: "For God has not given us a spirit of fear, but of power and of love and of a sound mind" (2 Timothy 1:7).

Challenge: Find and write out the definition of "sound mind" on a Post-It note. Place the note somewhere as a reminder of what is available to you twenty-four hours a day.

Declaration: The first time you read the declaration point to your mind, the second time point to your heart. "The spirit of fear must go in the name of Jesus. Fear does not belong to me. God has given me his power, love, and a sound mind. Jesus has given me peace of mind."

Prayer: "I exchange my fear for your peace. I give you my confused mind and receive a sound mind. I want your thoughts to become my thoughts and your way of thinking to become my way of thinking. Thank you for giving me your peace."

> "Peace I leave with you, My peace I give to you; not as the world gives do I give to you. Let not your heart be troubled, neither let it be afraid." (John 14:27)

Meditation and journaling: What fears are you struggling with today? Write them down in one column, and in a second column, write down what the Lord has given you to replace them.

Notes

Day 23

BEAUTIFUL, WONDERFUL YOU

I have given you beautiful eyes so you can see others through the eyes of the Spirit as I do. Your lovely mouth was created to speak gentle words of kindness and encouragement to those around you. I've adorned your neck with grace to stand fast on my principles and desires. Your feet have been anointed to carry the gospel and lead you on paths of righteousness for my namesake. I have given you a compassionate voice that can touch hard hearts and melt fears. Your delicate hands were created to reach out to the needy, the widow, and the orphan. Oh, my daughter, you are lovely, one of a kind, fearfully and wonderfully made.

Scripture: "O my dove, in the clefts of the rock, in the secret places of the cliff, let me see your face, let me hear your voice; for your voice is sweet, and your face is lovely" (Song of Solomon 2:14).

Challenge: Purchase a small item that describes what it means to be lovely. Place this token in the place where you have your quiet time with God.

Declaration: "The Lord says I am lovely in his sight. Every part of my body is fearfully and wonderfully made. I am one of a kind!"

Prayer: "It takes my breath away to recall the stunning words you have spoken to me. It is a challenge to think of myself as lovely, so help me to receive with joy and excitement all that you say about me. Thank you for creating me with attributes to glorify you."

Meditation and journaling: Read the devotional again, this time concentrate on the points which stand out to you the most. List them and explain why you feel this way.

Notes

Day 24

AN EXHIBIT OF CHRIST

My child, although you may not realize it, you are a temple of God because my Spirit dwells in you. You opened the door to me, and I have taken up residence in you.

Value and respect the truth that your "physical being" houses the essence of who I am. Take your everyday life - your sleeping, eating, going-to-work, and walking-around life and place it before me as an offering. You are my holy "cathedral" and set apart for my purposes by the Holy Spirit. Do you see what an honor and privilege it is to be an accurate reflection of me each day wherever you go? You bring my love, wisdom, encouragement and peace into every situation. How I long to give you an understanding of what this truly means so you can live in full assurance that you are indeed a temple of the living God! You belong to me and are precious, treasured, and loved more than you'll ever know.

Scripture: "Do you not know that you are the temple of God and that the Spirit of God dwells in you?" (1 Corinthians 3:16).

"Or do you not know that your body is the temple of the
Holy Spirit who is in you, whom you have from God, and
you are not your own?" (1 Corinthians 6:19).

Challenge: Ask the Lord if there are any changes he wants you to
make when it comes to caring for your body (regarding your eating,
exercising, sleeping, and life style.)

"I beseech you therefore, brethren, by the mercies of God,
that you present your bodies a living sacrifice, holy,
acceptable to God, which is your reasonable service."
(Romans 12:1)

Declaration: "My body is a temple of the living God. I will honor
and respect the truth that his Spirit lives in me!"

Prayer: "Lord, give me a deeper understanding of what it means to be
a temple of the Holy Spirit. I desire to honor the Spirit living in me.
Forgive me for not taking better care of my body. Empower me to
take the steps necessary to be a healthy and pure vessel of honor.
Thank you for the privilege of housing your Spirit."

Meditation and journaling: Think for a moment about the fact that
you carry God's presence inside you. Does this change the way you see
yourself? Write down your thoughts. How does it affect what you
watch, listen to, put in or on your body? Journal the changes you want
to make.

Notes

Understanding: Beryl

"And you shall put settings of stones in it, four rows of stones: The first row shall be a sardius, a topaz, and an emerald; this shall be the first row; the second row shall be a turquoise, a sapphire, and a diamond; the third row, a jacinth [ligure], an agate, and an amethyst; and the fourth row, a beryl, an onyx, and a jasper. They shall be set in gold settings." (Exodus 28:17–20)

Beryl is often referred to as the "mother of all gemstones" because it can be found in a wide range of colors, including blue, green, yellow, pink, and red. The word "beryl" means tarshish which indicates "refinery." This stone represents God's amazing work of refining us into his image by teaching us to make good decisions in order to live according to his ways.

"But who can endure the day of his coming? And who can stand when he appears? For he is like a refiner's fire and like launderers' soap. He will sit as a refiner and a purifier of silver" (Malachi 3:2–3).

This gem was given to the tribe of Dan. The name Dan means "God has judged me." The Word of God is our final authority when it comes to distinguishing between right and wrong. The Word also helps us judge whether we heard from God or not. God will never tell us to do something that contradicts his Word.

Charles Robinson, author of Stones of Real Value, says it perfectly: "Life is not full of mistakes as some would like to believe. Instead life is intimately ordained for each individual with causes and effects that are designed to purge our lives of the dross, so we can be more like Christ."

> "For You, O God, have tested us; You have refined us as
>
> silver is refined." (Psalm 66:10)

God's greatest desire is for us to be as a precious gem worthy to represent him to others. Aren't you elated at the thought that he refines and polishes us until we are beautiful stones able to make our mark on the earth today?

Day 25

FIERCELY PROTECTED

Though you may not believe it, I am protecting your heart, my daughter. It is a lie from the enemy that I withhold good things from you. The truth is, I have been shielding you from pain and suffering.

There are times when you rebel and fight against my will because I don't allow certain people or situations into your life. You are not all knowing, whereas I can see the pitfalls and snares up ahead.

I am your loving Heavenly Father, my daughter. You are dear to me. Let me be your protector. I will hide you from the enemy. I will set a guard around you to keep you from making wrong decisions out of desperation or unhealthy desires. When you yield your heart to me, I will keep you safe and secure. I will keep your will, mind, and emotions in check. Come to the one who is your shield and great reward. You can trust me!

Scripture: "He who dwells in the secret place of the Most High shall abide under the shadow of the Almighty. I will say of the Lord, 'He is my refuge and my fortress; my God, in him I will trust.' Surely he shall deliver you from the snare of the fowler and from the perilous pestilence. He shall cover you with his feathers, and under his wings you shall take refuge; his truth shall be your shield and buckler" (Psalm 91:1–4).

Challenge: Be truly honest. Has God shown you a person or situation you need to separate yourself from or forsake because they compromise your faith? Will you run to God for deliverance and direction?

Declaration: "The Lord is my protector! I will yield my life, future, safety and relationships to him. He knows what is best! I can trust him with my heart."

Prayer: "Forgive me, Lord, for resisting your perfect will by demanding my way which has caused unnecessary emotional pain and suffering. Continue to expose in me wrong thinking and unhealthy desires. I yield myself to you. In Jesus' name."

Meditation and journaling: Take time to ponder the truth you learned today. Journal what it means to you. List the names of people and situations you need to yield to the Lord.

Notes

Day 26

GENUINE FULFILLMENT

I know you seek fulfillment. You sometimes feel inadequate and incomplete. The truth is true fulfillment can only be found in pursuing and knowing me, the one who designed and created you. When you are connected to me, as a branch is connected to the vine, you are complete. Apart from me you can do nothing. I am your source, sufficiency and proficiency. Why do you seek fulfillment elsewhere? Why do you keep searching and grasping for things that will never satisfy? I am the only one who can satisfy your longing.

Let me develop your gifts and talents to walk in the destiny I have for you. The world can't offer you anything close to what I freely give.

Spend time with me. I will reveal a clearer picture of your true self. You will discover who you really are—my daughter, loved, cherished, and equipped to do good works. Embrace what's already inside you, placed there by me, your Creator.

Scripture: "…that the man [woman] of God may be complete, thoroughly equipped for every good work" (2 Timothy 3:17).

"Not that we are sufficient of ourselves to think of anything as being from ourselves, but our sufficiency is from God" (2 Corinthians 3:5).

Declaration: "My fulfillment is in you, Lord. You are more than enough for me! I am complete in you. I am loved, cherished and equipped to do good works."

Challenge: Keep track of your time today. Write down how much time you spend on things that are:

➤ Repetitive (work, church, family and exercise)

➤ Free time

➤ Potential time-wasters (social media, watching television, games, and surfing on the Internet).

Where do you need to make adjustments?

Prayer: "Father, I give you this longing for fulfillment which only you can satisfy. Show me who I am in you and the good works you have planned for me to walk in. Develop the gifts and talents you have placed within me. Help me stay connected to you. You are everything I need, my source. Apart from you I can do nothing."

Meditation and journaling: Ask yourself, "Am I striving for success, fame, acceptance or the approval of others? How much of my time and energy is spent on these things?" Now record the "why" behind your answer. Ask the Lord to give you a revelation of what it looks like to be complete, fulfilled, and satisfied in him alone. Journal what he reveals to you.

Notes

I Am Equipped For
Every Good Work

Day 27

TRUE WEALTH

My daughter, happiness is not found in earthly riches. You know deep down in your heart this is true. How many miserable wealthy people do you know—always seeking but never obtaining true happiness? You see the love of money brings trouble, nothing but trouble. Greed brings many sorrows. More money is not the answer to your problems. Don't love the world's goods. Love of the world squeezes out your love for me. Let this truth change your focus, putting to rest this issue forever.

True riches are already available to you: joy, peace, security, hope, love, wisdom, understanding, courage, and anything else you need whether emotional, physical, or spiritual. You are an heir to everything I've given my son, Jesus.

Come to me, run to me, and repent of your wanting, wanting, wanting. Yes, I desire to bless and provide for you financially, but let me change your heart. I love you! You can't imagine all of the good things I have prepared for you.

Scripture: "Command those who are rich in this present world not to be arrogant nor to put their hope in wealth, which is so uncertain, but to put their hope in God, who richly provides us with everything for our enjoyment" (1 Timothy 6:17 NIV).

"Eye has not seen, nor ear heard, nor have entered into the heart of man the things which God has prepared for those who love Him" (1 Corinthians 2:9).

Challenge: Invite the Holy Spirit to show you the true riches you need for this season of your life. Write them down in your journal and use the list as your daily prayer guide.

Declaration: "The Lord will provide for all my needs, in every area of life. He is the giver and desires to bless me. I am truly rich!"

Prayer: "I confess there are things of this world that I desire greatly to possess. Today I choose to lay them at your feet, Lord. I offer them as a sacrifice of worship. Do with them as you see fit. Give me a heart to pursue true riches. Thank you for providing everything I need. I love you, Lord."

Meditation and journaling: Spend some time thinking about the physical things you desire. Write these items in one column. Picture yourself laying them at the feet of Jesus. Make another column and write Scriptures about God's provision and true riches in exchange for these desires.

Notes

Day 28

BREAKING FREE

Don't surrender to the negative emotions and sins trying to enslave you. These bondages take, take, and take. They take everything you have, take advantage of you, take control of everything, and take away your freedom.

Freedom is yours for the asking. You only need to receive it. Freedom from the bondage of fear is yours. Experience my courage and the boldness of a lioness. Freedom from tormenting thoughts is yours. Experience my peace and the quietness of a dove. Freedom from the stronghold of worry is yours. Experience trust in me like the simple faith of a child.

Bondages must bow in my presence. Where my spirit is, there is freedom. Why not step out and trust me for the freedom you need today? Come and receive what is rightfully yours.

Scripture: "Therefore if the Son makes you free, you shall be free indeed" (John 8:36).

"Now the Lord is the Spirit, and where the Spirit of the Lord is, there is freedom" (2 Corinthians 3:17 NIV).

Challenge: Create a poster or design a notecard using the verses above. Place your artwork where you will see it all the time.

Declaration: "I am free from [fill in the blank]! Freedom is a gift, and it is rightfully mine! Jesus has set me free so I am free!"

Prayer: "Lord, I give you the emotions and sins that have enslaved and bound me like chains. Holy Spirit, come and set me free. I receive your deliverance and freedom. In Jesus' name."

Meditation and journaling: Ponder the areas where you need freedom. Write these down in detail. Start thanking God for delivering you from each one.

Notes

UNDERSTAND: AGATE

"And you shall put settings of stones in it, four rows of stones: The first row shall be a sardius, a topaz, and an emerald; this shall be the first row; the second row shall be a turquoise, a sapphire, and a diamond; the third row, a jacinth [ligure], an agate, and an amethyst; and the fourth row, a beryl, an onyx, and a jasper. They shall be set in gold settings." (Exodus 28:17–20)

The word "agate" implies something that separates light into flashes or streamers when introduced to a flame or spark. If an agate is placed in fire, it also gives off a sweet odor like that of myrrh.

In the "furnace of affliction", men like Joseph, King David, and the Apostle Paul gave off a sweet fragrance to the Lord by holding onto their faith in God and praising Him. We should follow their example by honoring God with a sacrifice of praise during our fiery trials and times of suffering. When we do, we give off a sweet, pleasing aroma unto the Lord, as well.

Agate represents the tribe of Manasseh. The meaning of Manasseh is "causing to forget." Joseph named his firstborn Manasseh because it meant "for God has made me forget all my toil and all my father's house" (Genesis 41:51).

There is much to learn about Joseph's life. The trials, setbacks, and disappointments he encountered did not stop him from trusting God in all circumstances. In fact, he said God had wiped away those hurtful memories. May these examples give us the courage to press on with the right attitude so we, too, can encourage others along the way.

Day 29

DESTINED TO MAKE A DIFFERENCE

I have chosen and appointed you to go into the world to bear fruit that lasts. My Word provides all the direction you need to walk in victory and power, but you must act on the things you learn. Be a doer of my Word not just a hearer.

I desire for my presence to be manifested, so broken lives can be healed and captives set free. I'm asking you to co-labor with me to reach those who need to hear the good news of my love and acceptance. Rest assured that I approve of you. You are my child. Humbly represent me to those who need a Savior and leave the results to me. As you are obedient to follow my instructions, you will walk in favor with those around you. Signs and wonders will follow you.

You are called. I equip the called. Seek me daily for instruction, courage, and strength. I will show you where to go and who to talk to, simply step out in faith. I will put my words in your mouth. Join me in this adventure! As I use you to reflect my glory, you will discover wonderful surprises around each corner.

Scripture: "You did not choose me, but I chose you and appointed you that you should go and bear fruit, and that your fruit should remain, that whatever you ask the Father in my name he may give you" (John 15:16).

Challenge: Step out in faith and find someone who needs prayer today (perhaps at the store, in the neighborhood, at work or at school). Ask if you can pray for them. Say a simple short prayer. Smile and trust God to do the rest.

Declaration: "I am appointed for good works. God approves of me. He will use me to bless others. It's not about what I do, but about what he can do as I step out in faith!"

Prayer: "Lord, I'm asking for boldness to co-labor with you so others can experience your love. Help me get my eyes off of myself and on to you and those around me who need encouragement. Open my ears to hear your instructions today. I believe with all my heart that you have chosen and appointed me even though I sometimes feel inadequate and nervous. Thank you for loving me and for allowing me to bear good fruit that will last."

Meditation and journaling: Re-read the devotion for today. Take the time to ponder the truth that God has appointed you and chosen you to bear good fruit. What part is hard to believe? What part is exciting to you? Record your thoughts.

Notes

$\mathcal{D}ay$ 30

HELP 24/7

My daughter, when you received the Holy Spirit, you received me, God on Earth, to live inside of you. Since that time, I have lived inside you, giving you all the help you need. I am telling you this so you will know the Holy Spirit is a real live person, your helper. He is not to be feared, but welcomed and heeded when he speaks to you. He will remind you of things I've already spoken to you and prepare you for things to come. He is your comforter and friend. The Spirit never forces you to do anything. Instead he gently and lovingly woos you into following him. It is his power behind your call or ministry, the one who equips you. He sticks closer than a brother, providing all the support you will ever need.

Scripture: "I will pray the Father, and he will give you another Helper, that he may abide with you forever" (John 14:16).

"But the Helper, the Holy Spirit, whom the Father will send in my name, he will teach you all things, and bring to your remembrance all things that I said to you" (John 14:26).

Challenge: Listen intently for the voice of the Holy Spirit today, ask him to show you who to bless today, as well as how to do it. Be open to what he tells you to do.

Declaration: "I have the Holy Spirit living inside of me. He is my comforter. He will give me all the help I need to complete my assignment here on earth. I receive His work in my life."

Prayer: "Lord, thank you for the Holy Spirit. Help me to reverence him in my life and not to quench or grieve him. I want to be sensitive to his voice and leading. I desire to grow in this truth, so reveal how he works in my life."

Meditation and journaling: Take time to ponder your thoughts regarding the Holy Spirit. Is this teaching new to you? How have you seen him working in and through your life? How do you see him now? Record your thoughts.

Notes

....

....

....

....

....

....

....

....

....

....

....

....

....

....

UNDERSTANDING: TOPAZ

"And you shall put settings of stones in it, four rows of stones: The first row shall be a sardius, a topaz, and an emerald; this shall be the first row; the second row shall be a turquoise, a sapphire, and a diamond; the third row, a jacinth [ligure], an agate, and an amethyst; and the fourth row, a beryl, an onyx, and a jasper. They shall be set in gold settings." (Exodus 28:17–20)

Although a biblical word study doesn't offer much information about topaz, Wikipedia says that this stone is basically colorless and transparent but sometimes displays hints of wine red, yellow, blue, and gold. It is even known to be opaque or translucent. "Topaz" means "to seek." Proverbs 8:17 tells us, "I love those who love me, and those who seek me diligently will find me." Our Lord is available every moment of every day. If we seek him, we will find him.

Topaz represents the tribe of Issachar. Issachar means "fire" and "he will bring a reward." Those people who desire to know the Lord will be rewarded. They will discover the treasure they seek. You only need to look for him. He is waiting to be found! Don't you find that encouraging?

I HAVE THE HOLY SPIRIT
Living Inside Of Me

CONCLUSION

Congratulations! You completed the 30-day search for your identity as a child of God, but the journey doesn't end here. You have an open invitation to continue the process of learning and growing into the beautiful masterpiece God created you to be. Rest assured that the Holy Spirit will continue to teach and instruct you in the days ahead and will remind you of the things you've learned. Allow your heart to be open to his gentle nudging to direct your steps. You have begun an exciting journey of discovery. The best is yet to come!

Visit my Facebook page at www.facebook.com/AuthorJaneLanders to share your comments after completing the journey or my Instagram account at landers_jane where you can give me a status update #nomoreindentitycrisis.

Here are a few suggestions to continue your journey in discovering who God created you to be:

www.gallupstrengthcenter.com

www.giftstest.com

Thank you for sharing this 30-day quest with me. May your heart be continually touched and nourished by the indescribable presence of God and the keen awareness of being a daughter of the Most High King!

If you have any questions or you would like to share your reaction to my book, please email me at janelanders@att.net.

REFERENCES

Unless otherwise noted, all scriptures are taken from the New King James Version Bible or The Message: The Bible in Contemporary Language, by Eugene H. Peterson

Stones of Real Value: On the Breastplate by Charles Robinson, Servants of the Savior International Ministries

Merriam Webster Online Dictionary

Wikipedia, The Free Encyclopedia

Countless hours of research, notes from personal journals, prayer, and meditation were my utmost tools by far, along with the best source of all, the Holy Spirit.

ABOUT THE AUTHOR

Over the years, Jane Landers has served as pastor's wife, administrator, teacher, children's ministry director and storyteller.

Jane completed the course on "How to Be a Clown" in 1991 at Yavapai College in Prescott, Arizona which launched her career as a.k.a. Bleenky the Clown.

She enjoys her flower garden, chatting with friends over tea, long morning walks with her husband, and spending time with her grandchildren.

Jane resides in Seminole, Texas with her husband, Shane. They have four beautiful daughters and eight delightful grandchildren.